SYMBOLS OF THE CHURCH

Revised Edition

Edited by
Carroll E. Whittemore

Drawings by
William Duncan

Abingdon Press

SYMBOLS OF THE CHURCH

Fifth Printing 1991

ISBN 0-687-18301-4

Printed in the United States of America

CONTENTS

SYMBOLS OF THE OLD AND NEW TESTAMENTS

ALPHA AND OMEGA
The first and last letters of the Greek alphabet which signify that Jesus is the beginning and the end of all things. (See the book of the Revelation, chapter 1, verse 8.)

ALPHA-MU-OMEGA
Another symbol for our Lord consists of the initial letters of Greek words for "yesterday, today, and forever." (See Hebrew 13:8.)

ALTAR AND CHERUBIM / ARK OF THE COVENANT
The Ark of the Covenant was the meeting place of God with the Israelites on the journey from Egypt and therefore was the symbol of the presence of God among them.

ALTAR OF BURNT OFFERING
The altar upon which the offerings of first-fruits and grains were made. Also a symbol for Old Testament worship.

ANGEL, HERALD
The angel floating in space with his right hand raised in benediction is a symbol of the Nativity.

ARK AND RAINBOW
The most common symbol of the flood. Also symbol of the church, since in the Ark all living creatures found refuge from danger.

THE ASCENSION
This subject is usually pictured, though sometimes Elijah's chariot of fire is employed as a symbol.

AUREOLE
An elongated nimbus used only as surrounding the entire body of our Lord, or the virgin and child.

BANNER
A banner is the symbol of rejoicing and of victory. The Lamb of God bearing a banner with a cross symbolizes the joyful victory over death won by our Lord.

BASIN. *See* Pitcher and Basin.

BEEHIVE
Symbol for a community of those who work together for the benefit of all. Used modernly as a symbol for the Christian Church, and is one of the best.

BELL
A bell calling people to worship symbolizes the need of priority for the things of God over the secular. In general, the sounding forth of the Word.

BIBLE, OPEN
Symbolizes the Word of God.

BIRDS AND GRAPES
From ancient classic times comes this motif often found on sarcophagi. It symbolizes the faithful feeding on the grapes, the blood of Christ.

BURNING BUSH
The burning bush that was not consumed is the symbol for the call of the great Hebrew leader, Moses, who recognized that God was speaking to him in that unusual place.

BUTTERFLY
Symbol of the resurrection and eternal life. As the butterfly leaves the pupa and soars upward with a new body, so through Jesus Christ are his followers borne to a new life.

CANDLE LIGHTED
These suggest our Lord's words, "I am the light of the world," John 8:12. They also represent his twofold nature—human and divine, when two candlesticks are used.

CANDLESTICK, SEVEN-BRANCH / MENORAH
The seven-branch candlestick is a symbol for Old Testament worship. It is known as the Menorah and is used in Jewish synagogues today.

CENSER
Symbol of prayer. As incense smoke wafts upward so prayer ascends before God (Revelation 8:4 and Psalm 141:2).

CHALICE. *See* Cup.

SYMBOLS OF THE OLD AND NEW TESTAMENTS

CHI RHO
A monogram of the first two letters, Chi (X) and Rho (P), of the Greek word for Christ.

CHI RHO WITH ALPHA AND OMEGA
This symbol for our Lord comes from the catacombs and indicates that he is the beginning, continuation, and end of all things.

CHI RHO IN JOINED RINGS
This is a fairly recent figure to symbolize matrimony. It signifies the joining of man and woman in unending union with the presence of Christ indicated by the Chi Rho monogram.

CHRIST THE KING (CHRISTUS REX)
When the Christ is depicted wearing Eucharistic vestments and as reigning from the cross this is known as the Crucifix of Christ the King.

CHRISTMAS ROSE
Symbol of the Nativity and of messianic prophecy, a white hardy rose that blooms at Christmas.

CIRCLE
Standing for eternity, because it is without beginning and without end.

CIRCLE AND TRIANGLE
Suggests the eternity of the Trinity.

CIRCLE CONTAINING THE CHI RHO WITH THE ALPHA AND OMEGA
Symbol for Christ is within symbol for eternity (circle), and so signifies the eternal existence of our Lord.

CIRCLE OF STARS WITH SUN AND MOON
Represents Jacob and wife and Jacob's twelve sons.

CIRCLES, THREE INTERTWINING
These indicate the doctrine of the equality, unity, and co-eternal nature of the three persons of the Trinity.

CLOVER / SHAMROCK
The prominent three leaves make the clover an easily understood symbol of the Trinity. Legend says St. Patrick used the clover to explain the Trinity in his preaching.

COAT AND DICE
One of the Passion symbols, referring to the garment of Jesus for which the soldiers at the foot of the cross cast lots (John 19:23-24).

THE COCK
The crowing of the cock is a warning to Peter as to his steadfastness of faith and as a rebuke to his weakness (Mark 14:72).

COINS. *See* Money Bag and Silver Coins.

COLUMBINE
The seven-petaled columbine blossom, or the seven-blossom stalk stand for the seven gifts of the Holy Spirit as given in Revelation 5:12: "power, and riches, and wisdom, and might, and honor, and glory, and blessing."

THE CORNERSTONE
The cornerstone with abbreviations of the Greek words for Jesus Christ symbolizes him who was declared to be the chief cornerstone (Ephesians 2:20).

ANCHOR CROSS
Used by the early Christians in the catacombs. Ancient Egyptian in its origin.

BETHLEHEM STAR CROSS WITH FLAMES
The central star shape represents the star that announced the birth of Christ. It is elongated into a cross to represent at the same time the cross on which Christ died. Surrounding the star cross are four flames that signify the tongues of fire of Pentecost.

BUDDED CROSS
It suggests the young or immature Christian, while the Cross Fleurée, or flowered cross, denotes by its more fully opened ends the adult Christian.

CALVARY CROSS
Sometimes called the Graded Cross. The three steps, from the top down, stand for faith, hope, love.

CELTIC CROSS
Or cross of Iona, dates back to early centuries of the Christian era. It was said to have been taken from what is now Ireland to the island of Iona by Columba in the sixth century.

CROSS AND CROWN
These symbolize the reward of the faithful in the life after death to those who believe in the crucified Savior.
"Be thou faithful unto death, and I will give thee a crown of life" (Revelation 2:10).

11

CROSS AND TRIANGLE
A symbol used mostly in church embroidery. Here the cross intertwined with the triangle emphasizes that Christ is one in the Holy Trinity.

CROSS CROSSLET
Four Latin crosses joined at their bases. Represents Christianity spreading in the four directions and is especially appropriate when the missionary idea is expressed.

CROSS FITCHÉE
Any cross whose lower arm is sharpened. This is said to have been used by the Crusaders who carried crosses with a pointed lower end which could be thrust into the ground easily at the time of devotions.

CROSS OF LORRAINE
Has two horizontal arms, a short one near the top and a longer one near the base.

CROSS OF TRIUMPH
Symbolic of the triumph of the gospel throughout the earth.

CROSS PATTÉE
Resembles the Maltese Cross. A beautiful form of the cross used widely for decorative purposes.

CROSS TREFFLÉE
A beautiful form with ends formed as trefoils. It is widely used wherever a decorative style of cross is needed. Also known as the Cross Botonnée.

EASTERN CROSS
The upper horizontal arm represents the place of the inscription over the head of the crucified Jesus. The lower slanting arm represents his footrest, since the Eastern Church believes Jesus was crucified with his feet side by side and not crossed one over the other as usually pictured by the Western Church.

GREEK CROSS
With all arms of equal length.

GREEK CROSS AND X MONOGRAM
In this symbol for our Lord a Greek cross is superimposed on a X (Chi), first letter of the Greek word for Christ.

GREEK CROSS WITH WORDS
Greek cross with abbreviated Greek words for Jesus Christ (abbreviations indicated by horizontal lines) and "nika" meaning "conquers": "Jesus Christ Conquers."

HUGUENOT CROSS
Used by the French Protestants of the sixteenth and seventeenth centuries known as Huguenots. Worn today by many French Protestants; often times only the dove is worn. To a Frenchman, if used complete or only the dove it signifies the wearer is a Protestant.

JERUSALEM OR CRUSADER'S CROSS
Usually has four small crosses between the arms, the five crosses symbolizing the five wounds of our Lord. Worn by Godfrey de Bouillon, first ruler of Jerusalem after the liberation from the Moslems.

LATIN CROSS
The most commonly used form of cross.

MALTESE CROSS
Consisting of four spearheads with points together. Dates back to the days of the Crusades when the order of the Hospitallers used it for their emblem. Later they made their headquarters on the island of Malta.

PAPAL CROSS
Has three horizontal arms, each a little longer than the other, in descending order. The two upper cross bars are said by some to signify the crosses of the two crucified beside our Lord. This cross is used only in Papal processions.

PATRIARCHAL CROSS
Has two horizontal arms, the upper one slightly shorter than the lower. The upper represents the inscription over the head of our Lord on the cross.

ST. ANDREW'S CROSS
Tradition says the apostle Andrew died on this form of cross, requesting that he be crucified on a cross unlike that of his Lord.

SWASTIKA
A pagan symbol used by early Christians in the catacombs. During the second and third centuries, some authorities say, the swastika was the only form of cross used by the Christians. It is made both clockwise and counter.

TAU CROSS
So-called because of resemblance to the Greek letter T. This is the original form of cross.

CROWN AND CROSS. *See* Cross and Crown.

THE CROWN OF THORNS
A mockery crown, symbol of humiliation and suffering, plaited by the soldiers and imposed upon Jesus during his trial before Pilate (John 19:2).

CUP
A symbol of the blood of Christ and of the sacrament of Holy Communion.

CYPRESS
The cypress has long been associated with death and is found in both pagan and Christian cemetaries. Once cut, it is said, the cypress never springs up again.

DAGGER AND SHIELD
The symbol of Abraham is the sacrificial knife, with God's promise to him indicated by a blue shield with many stars. One large star stands for the Messiah.

DAISY
Conventionalized, symbol of the innocence of the Holy Child. Popular usage started toward the end of the fifteenth century.

DISTAFF AND YARN
The symbol for Eve, the first woman according to the biblical account, is a distaff.

DOORPOSTS AND LINTEL
The blood-sprinkled doorposts with lintel is a symbol of God's protection in Egypt at the passing over of the destroying angel, which is central in the Passover Festival.

DOVE
The dove expresses innocence and purity. It signifies the Holy Spirit and the presence of God as hovering over the water at creation, and above Jesus at his baptism.

DOVES, SEVEN
Seven doves surrounding a circle containing the two letters SS (Sanctus Spiritus, Latin for Holy Spirit) symbolize the seven gifts of the Holy Spirit, as given in Revelation 5:12.

DOVE WITH OLIVE SPRIG
Sometimes used as a symbol for the flood. It denotes peace, forgiveness, and anticipation of new life.

DRAGON
A symbol for Satan and also, sin and pestilence. When shown underfoot it signifies victory over evil.

EAGLE
The high-soaring eagle is the emblem of John because in his narrative he rises to the loftiest heights in dealing with the mind of Christ.

EWER. *See* Pitcher and Basin.

EYE IN THE TRIANGLE / THE ALL-SEEING EYE
This all-seeing eye of God looks out from the triangle of the Trinity. It is found on some English and Greek churches.

FISH
A secret sign used by the early persecuted Christians to designate themselves as believers in Jesus. The initial letters of the Greek words for "Jesus Christ, God's Son, Savior," spell the Greek word for fish.

ΙΧΘΥC

FISH, THREE IN A CIRCLE
The fish is an ancient symbol for our Lord, and three fish in a circle signify that man's salvation comes from the Triune God.

FLAMES
Flames or fire are often used in the Bible to signify an appearance of God to man. The burning bush in Exodus is an Old Testament example. In Acts 2:3 "tongues as of fire" appeared on the heads of the disciples at Pentecost, signifying the descent of the Holy Spirit.

FLEUR DE LIS
One of the most popular symbols for Mary. It was selected by the French kings as their symbol and later was used in the banner of Jeanne d'Arc.

FOOT
The human foot moves in the dust of the earth and so symbolizes humility and voluntary servitude.

GRAPES
A bunch of grapes signifies the sacrament of the Holy Communion, and is most appropriately found about the Communion table.

GRIFFIN
The Griffin, an imaginary creature with the wings and beak of an eagle and the body of a lion, suggests the twofold nature of Christ. The eagle portion recalls his divine nature and the lion portion denotes his humanity.

HALO. *See* Nimbus.

HAND OF GOD, BLESSER
Symbol of the Father, as blesser. The three extended fingers suggest the Holy Trinity, while the two closed fingers denote the twofold nature of the Son.

HAND OF GOD, CREATOR
Symbol of the Father, with the idea of creator (Genesis 1:1). The tri-radiant nimbus denotes the hand of the Divine.

HAND OF GOD / SOULS OF THE RIGHTEOUS
Symbolizes a sentence in the Book of Wisdom, "The souls of the righteous are in the hand of God."

HARP
The symbol for music, especially that rendered in praise of God.

HARP AND LION
Symbolize David because of his skill as a musician and his exploits in protecting his sheep as a shepherd boy.

HAWTHORN OR GLASTONBURY THORN

A thornwood tree which blossoms at Christmas. According to legend Joseph of Arimathaea struck his thornwood staff into the earth and it later miraculously blossomed at the time of Christ's birth. Symbol of the Nativity; named because of the ancient tree, offshoots of which still grow within the grounds of the ruined abbey of Glastonbury, England.

HEART, PIERCED BY DAGGER

A symbol for Mary, the mother of Jesus, because of the prophecy uttered by the aged Simeon in the Temple, "Yea, and a sword shall pierce through thine own soul" (Luke 2:35).

HERALD ANGEL. *See* Angel.

HOLLY

The thorny, prickly leaves of the holly tree are regarded as a symbol of the crown of thorns, and so recalls the Passion of Christ.

IESUS MONOGRAM

Formed by using the first two and last letters of the word for Jesus in Greek, with abbreviation sign.

THE IHS

Are the first three letters (iota, eta, sigma) of the Greek spelling of Jesus. The upper form is the more ancient, though the lower is the more common now.

I.N.R.I.

Initial letters for Latin superscription on the cross: Iesus Nazarenus Rex Iudaeorum, Jesus of Nazareth, King of the Jews (John 19:19).

IRIS
Frequently used instead of the lily in pictures of Mary, the mother of Jesus.

I X MONOGRAM
This symbol for our Lord consists of the initial letters for the Greek words for Jesus Christ arranged as a monogram.

THE JESSE TREE
The Jesse Tree symbol is derived from Isaiah 11:1, "And there shall come forth a rod out of the stem of Jesse, and a Branch shall grow out of his roots." It is a symbol designed to recall the greatness of the contribution Jesse made under the plan of God.

LADDER CROSSED WITH REED AND SPONGE
A symbol of our Lord's crucifixion, since the sponge was used to provide him vinegar while on the cross (Matthew 27:48).

LAMB
The blood of a lamb without blemish was commanded by God to be sprinkled on the doorposts of Hebrew homes in Egypt so his destroying angel might pass over and spare Israel. This was memorialized in the Passover Festival. In the New Testament, the lamb is often used figuratively to symbolize Christ and his sacrifice.

LAMB AND BOOK
Revelation 5:1. The lamb is reclining on the Book of the Seven Seals, reclining because he is the Wounded Lamb. The three-rayed nimbus denotes deity.

LAMB STANDING WITH THE BANNER OF VICTORY
No longer wounded, but standing with the banner of victory, suggesting the victorious nature of his sacrifice.

LAMP
A symbol for the Word of God. Probably coming from "Thy word is a lamp unto my feet" (Psalm 119:105).

LAMPS, SEVEN
The seven lamps burning before the throne of God (Revelation 4:5) symbolize the Holy Spirit. Occasionally seven flames alone are used.

THE LILY
Symbol of Easter and immortality. The bulb decays in the ground, yet from it new life is released.

LILY OF THE VALLEY
This sweet blossom signifies humility and purity, and is used most frequently wih Mary the Mother of Jesus, or with Jesus himself.

LINTEL. *See* Doorposts and Lintel.

LION, WINGED
The symbol for Mark because his Gospel narrative begins with, "The voice of one crying in the wilderness," and this suggests the roar of a lion.

LOTUS. *See* Water Lily.

MANGER
Suggestive of the simplicity of poverty surrounding the birth of Jesus and typical of his entire life.

MENORAH. *See* Candlestick, Seven-Branch.

MONEY BAG AND SILVER COINS
Emblem of the treachery of Judas in his conspiracy between the chief priests and himself for the betrayal of Jesus (Matthew 26:15).

MYRTLE
From early times myrtle has been the symbol of love. In Christian symbolism it is an allusion to the Gentiles who became followers of Christ.

NAILS
The great nails driven through the palms and the feet of Jesus at his crucifixion are symbols of the poignancy of his physical suffering (John 19:17-18).

NIMBUS
The nimbus has come to be emblematic of sanctity and to denote a person recognized for unusual piety, such as, apostles, martyrs, and saints.

NIMBUS, THREE-RAYED
Signifies divinity and is used only with any Person of the Trinity. Rays of light were ancient emblems of divine power.

OLIVE BRANCH
Since olive trees provide shelter and opportunity for rest, and the olive oil is used for ointments, the olive branch is the symbol for peace, harmony, and healing.

OX
Suggestive of strength, patience, and sacrifice, and for this reason a symbol of our Redeemer. "For my yoke is easy, and my burden is light" (Matthew 11:30).

OX, WINGED
Luke is symbolized by the ox, the animal of sacrifice, since Luke stresses the atoning sacrifice of Jesus.

PAX
The Latin word for peace.

PALM BRANCH
Branches of the palm tree, regarded as sacred from early Semitic times, were carried by the Jews as a sign of triumphant rejoicing (John 12:13).

PEACOCK
Early symbol of the Resurrection. When the peacock sheds his feathers, he grows more brilliant ones than those he lost.

PELICAN
Symbol of the Atonement. Pelican was believed to draw blood from its own breast to feed its young.

PHOENIX

A mythical bird which at death bursts into flame but rises from its own ashes. Symbol of the Resurrection and immortal life.

PITCHER AND BASIN

Emblem of the footwashing ceremony recorded in John 13:5—evidence of the humility of Christ's love and his estimate of true greatness in his kingdom.

POMEGRANATE

Symbol of the Resurrection and the power of our Lord, who was able to burst the tomb and come forth.

POPPY

The poppy signifies sleep, ignorance, and indifference. Sometimes shown with reference to the Passion of Christ because of the inference of sleep and death.

ROSE. *See* Christmas Rose.

ROOSTER. *See* Cock.

SCOURGE AND PILLAR

The scourge is a symbol of the Passion and is sometimes accompanied by a pillar to which any unfortunate victim may have been tied.

SCROLL
The scroll stands for the five Books of Moses, as the first five books of the Old Testament are commonly called. These are known as the Torah and constitute the most sacred Law of the Jews.

SERPENT AND APPLE
The serpent representing Satan is coiled about the trunk of a tree, with the apple as the object of temptation.

SERPENT AND WORLD
The sinful nature of humankind everywhere as a result of Adam's fall is traditionally represented by a serpent coiled around the earth.

SHAMROCK. *See* Clover.

SHELL WITH DROPS OF WATER
A symbol of our Lord's baptism.

THE SHEPHERD AND LAMB
This symbol, found in the catacombs, calls to mind the loving care of Jesus, the Good Shepherd.

SHIELD OF THE TRINITY
The three curving sides, each exactly equal in length, carry the Latin words "is not." The short straight bands have the word "is." The outer circles bear the words "Father," "Son," "Holy Spirit," while the inner circle is "God."

SKELETON
Obviousy the symbol of death. Frequently shown with a scythe, since death is the cutting of this life, and/or an hourglass the symbol of the passing of time.

SKULL
A skull lying at the foot of the cross represents the skull of Adam and symbolizes the sin of humankind where blood from the Lamb of God can drip upon it and wash away the believer's sin.

SMOKE. *See* Censer.

STAR OF DAVID
Two interwoven equilateral triangles for a six-pointed star traditionally the shape of David's shield. Sometimes called "the Creator's Star," the six points recall the six days of creation.

STAR, EPIPHANY
The star of Jacob (Numbers 24:17) finds its fulfillment in the "manifestation" of Jesus to the Gentiles (Matthew 2:1-2).

STAR, NINE-POINTED
The nine points of this star stand for the nine fruits of the spirit as found in Galatians 5:22. Usually each point contains the name or initial of the Latin word of the gift it symbolizes.

THE STORK
Symbolizes chastity, prudence, and vigilence. Associated with the Annunciation because, as the stork announces the coming of spring, the Annunciation to Mary indicated the Advent of Christ.

SUN AND IHC
Made up of the Iesugram symbol placed in the circle of eternity and with flames shooting out in every direction. Suggests the "Sun of Righteousness" mentioned in Malachi 4:2.

SWAN
The swan is the symbol of a hypocrite because its beautiful white plumage covers its black flesh beneath.

SWORD, FLAMING
Symbolizes the flaming sword which guarded the path to the tree of life after the expulsion of Adam from the Garden of Eden.

TABLETS OF STONE WITH THE TEN COMMANDMENTS
Represented by a twofold stone tablet. The Roman Catholic Church and the Lutheran bodies show the first table and three commandments and the second with seven commandments.

TABLETS OF STONE WITH THE TEN COMMANDMENTS
Other bodies of the church show four numbers for the first table and six on the second table. Sometimes five numbers on each table are used.

THORNS. *See* Crown of Thorns.

TORCH, BURNING
As a Christian symbol it signifies witnessing for Christ. "Let you light so shine" (Matthew 5:16).

SYMBOLS OF THE OLD AND NEW TESTAMENTS

TREFOIL
A symbol of the Trinity.

TRIANGLE, EQUILATERAL
Symbol of the Trinity. The three distinct angles combine to make one complete figure.

TRIANGLE WITH EYE. *See* Eye in the Triangle.

THE TRIQUETRA
Early symbol of the Holy Trinity. The three equal arcs express eternity in their continuous form, indivisibility in their interweaving, and their center is a triangle, ancient Trinity symbol.

THE TRIQUETRA AND CIRCLE
The Triquetra, denoting the Blessed Trinity, is combined with the circle of eternity producing a figure recalling several spiritual truths.

TRUMPET
Symbol for the day of judgment, the resurrection, and the call to worship.

TRUMPET AND SWORD
Symbols of Joshua who brought down the walls of Jericho to the accompaniment of the sound of trumpets.

UNICORN
A familiar symbol of our Lord; early accepted as a symbol of purity and therefore especially related to the virgin and the birth of Jesus.

VIOLET
St. Bernard describes the Virgin Mary as "the violet of humility." The violet is also used to evince the humility of the Son of God in assuming human form.

WATER LILY/LOTUS
This blossom of exquisite beauty and purity, with its roots in the mud, suggests that the life of the Christian may rise through and above unlovely and evil influences.

WHEAT
Heads of wheat symbolize the Bread of Life (Mark 14:22). With clusters of grapes, appropriate for holy tables.

WINGED MAN
The winged man represents Matthew because his Gospel narrative traces Jesus' human genealogy.

WINGS
Wings symbolize a divine mission, so angels and cherubim are shown with wings. The four evangelists are often shown as winged creatures.

XP. *See* Chi Rho.

SYMBOLS OF THE APOSTLES

PETER
The crossed keys recall Peter's confession and our Lord's gift to him of the keys of the kingdom. (See Matthew 16:18-19).

ANDREW
Tradition says that while Andrew was preaching in Greece he was put to death on a cross of this type.

JAMES (THE GREATER)
The scallop shell is the symbol of pilgrimage and stands for this apostle's zeal and missionary spirit.

JOHN, AS AN APOSTLE
Early writers state that John once drank from a poisoned chalice and was unharmed. Jesus once said that John should drink of his cup.

PHILIP
A cross and two loaves of bread, because of Philip's remark when Jesus fed the multitude (John 6:7).

JUDE
This apostle traveled far on missionary jouneys in company with Simon, according to tradition, hence the ship.

JAMES (THE LESSER)
Represented by a saw, since it is said his body was sawn asunder after a horrible martyrdom.

MATTHEW, AS AN APOSTLE
Is symbolized by three purses referring to his original calling as a tax collector.

THOMAS
A carpenter's square and a spear, because this apostle is said to have built a church in India with his own hands. Later, he was persecuted there and was killed with a spear by a pagan priest.

BARTHOLOMEW
This apostle is said to have been flayed alive, hence he is usually represented by three flaying knives.

SIMON THE ZEALOT
This symbol is a book upon which rests a fish, because through the power of the gospel Simon became a great fisher of men.

MATTHIAS
Chosen to take the place of Judas, he is symbolized by an open Bible and double-bladed battle-ax. He is said to have been beheaded after his missionary work.

THE TWELVE APOSTLES
The apostles have been symbolized as a group as well as individually. In one place, twelve doves are used; in another, twelve men are shown, each with a sheep. Some very early carvings represent the apostles as twelve sheep.

SYMBOLS OF THE APOSTLES

PAUL
Referred to as the "Apostles to the Gentiles," but not one of the twelve apostles. Symbolized by an open Bible with the words "Spiritus Gladius" (sword of the Spirit), and behind the Bible the sword of the Spirit itself.

BARNABAS
Included among the apostles, although like Paul he was not one of the Twelve. Tradition says he was especially successful as a preacher, hence the Gospel in the symbol.

OTHER SYMBOLS OF THE APOSTLES

Peter

Philip

Thomas

Andrew

Jude

Bartholomew

James the Greater

James the Less

Simon

John, an Apostle

Matthew, an Apostle

Matthias

SYMBOLS OF SAINTS

ST. AGATHA
Born in a noble Sicilian family, Agatha was famous for her beauty and gentleness. She refused to give up her Christian faith at the command of the governor, and she was unspeakably tortured. She is the patroness of bell-founders. Died A.D. 251.

ST. AGNES
She was a devoted follower of Jesus who steadfastly refused all offers of marriage, claiming she was the "bride of Christ." She is now considered the patroness of chastity. Martyred about A.D. 304.

ST. AIDAN
An Irish monk of Iona who was sent to evangelize northern England and received the devoted help of Kings Oswald and Oswin. Died A.D. 651.

ST. ALBAN
He was a pagan who sheltered a persecuted priest, and was converted. He helped the priest escape, whereupon the fury of the pagans turned on Alban. He was beheaded in the city which now bears his name. Martyred about A.D. 303.

ST. AMBROSE
This famous Bishop of Milan, one of the four doctors of the Western Church, was a great lover of music. He added to the richness of sacred services of the church with it and introduced the antiphonal chants bearing his name today. Died A.D. 397.

ST. ANNE
The mother of the Virgin Mary. From the Apocryphal Gospel records Anne has been honored, though nothing is known of her life. The book is a symbol of her careful instruction of Mary. First Century.

ST. ANTHONY OF PADUA
A faithful and eloquent preacher against doctrinal errors and wickedness, he is usually referred to as the "hammer of heretics." A follower of St. Francis, he preached in France, Italy, and Sicily until his death in Padua. Died A.D. 1231.

ST. ATHANASIUS
Athanasius was bishop of Alexandria and an unusual student of Holy Scriptures. He was an authority on the ecclesiastical and canon laws of the church and exerted a powerful influence in the church. Died A.D. 373.

ST. AUGUSTINE
Known as the "Apostle of the English," Augustine and forty monks carried the gospel to England. Received by the pagan king, Ethelbert, who soon was baptized with many others. Later Augustine was made bishop. died A.D. 604.

ST. AUGUSTINE OF HIPPO
His virtuous life and brilliant intellect caused him to be elected to the See of Hippo where he was recognized as the pillar of Orthodox Christianity. His *Confessions* and *City of God* have greatly influenced religious thinking. A.D. 354–430.

ST. BASIL
A bishop in Asia Minor, where he defended his province against the Arian heresy. He wrote many doctrinal works, founded the first recorded hospice for travelers, and wrote the Eucharistic liturgy which bears his name. Died A.D. 379.

ST. BEDE
The Venerable Bede entered a monastery at the age of seven years for his education and remained there for the rest of his life. He spent his time reading, praying, teaching, and writing. Died A.D. 735.

ST. BERNARD
Early joined the Cistercians and later founded the Abbey of Clairvaux. Bernard was the advisor of popes and kings and wrote profusely, especially on the love of God. Died A.D. 1153.

ST. BONIFACE
This saint, a Benedictine monk, carried the gospel to Germany and founded the Abbey of Fulda which was the center of German missionary activity. Martyred A.D. 755.

ST. BRIDE (ST. BRIDGET)
Baptized by St. Patrick, St. Bridget founded the first nunnery in Ireland. Legends stress her mercy and pity for the poor. Died A.D. 523.

— music

ST. CECILIA
This Roman lady, educated as a Christian, converted her husband and shared martyrdom with him. Tradition says she wrote hymns and sang beautifully so she is regarded as the patroness of music. Martyred about A.D. 200.

ST. CHARLES (KING CHARLES THE FIRST)
The only person formally canonized by the English Church since the Reformation. Known as Charles the Martyr, he was beheaded in London in 1649.

ST. CHRISTOPHER
Legend says that Offero (bearer) once carried the Christ Child on his shoulders across a swollen stream, and so thereafter was known as Christopher (Christ-bearer). Patron saint of travel. Martyred about A.D. 250.

ST. CHRYSOSTOM
John, bishop of Constantinople became the most eloquent preacher of the early church, and so was called Chrysostom, or Golden-mouthed. Legend says that when he was a baby a swarm of bees settled on his mouth. Died A.D. 407.

ST. CLARE
Moved by the influence of St. Francis, she gave herself to monastic life and founded the order of the "Poor Clares." Her great charity and spiritual devotion have won the admiration of all. Died A.D. 1253.

ST. CLEMENT
Converted to the Christian faith by St. Paul. He became the bishop of Rome, later he was martyred by being cast into the sea tied to an anchor. Martyred about A.D. 100.

ST. COLUMBA (ST. COLUM)
This saint founded many churches and monasteries in Ireland and Scotland, the most famous of which was on the island of Iona. One of the most consecrated and indefatigable of Christian missionaries. Died A.D. 597.

ST. CUTHBERT
A shepherd boy in Britain who embraced the monastic life. He became a faithful preacher and missionary to the wild and untamed mountain people of Scotland and on the island of Farne. Died A.D. 687.

ST. CYRIL OF JERUSALEM
Bishop of Jerusalem for many years. At one time was expelled because he sold ornaments of the church to provide food for the poor. Wrote instructions on Christian doctrine for catechumens which have been highly regarded ever since. Died A.D. 386.

ST. CYRIL OF ALEXANDRIA
A native of Alexandria and patriarch of the city. Gave much of his life to defense of the truth of Christ's divinity. Died A.D. 444.

ST. CYPRIAN
A lawyer, converted to Christianity, became the bishop of Carthage. Wrote several important theological treatises and became a pioneer of Christian liturature writing. Martyred A.D. 258.

ST. DOMINIC
Born a nobleman of Spain he resigned all worldly honors for his Master. He established the Dominican order of Preaching Friars, and did not spare himself in his work for the glory of God. Died A.D. 1221.

ST. DUNSTAN
The English-born Dunstan became Abbot of Glastonbury. Legend says the devil went to Dunstan's cell to tempt him, whereupon Dunstan caught the devil by the nose with red-hot pincers and caused him to flee. Died A.D. 988.

ST. EDWARD THE MARTYR
King of England at the age of thirteen. He was stabbed to death by his stepmother, who wanted the throne for her own son Ethelred. Martyred A.D. 979.

ST. ELIZABETH
The mother of John the Baptist. All that is known of her is given in the first chapter of Luke. First century.

ST. FRANCIS
The well-born Francis resolved to devote his life to God. Founded the Franciscans, the members of which embrace complete poverty, and help the sick and suffering. Died A.D. 1226.

ST. GABRIEL
This archangel was sent to Mary to announce that she was to be the mother of Jesus. He is sometimes called the "Angel of the Annunciation" (Luke 1).

ST. GEORGE
St. George is the patron saint of England and venerated as the model of knighthood and protector of women. Also the patron of soldiers since he was long a military man engaged in warfare with the pagans. Martyred A.D. 303.

ST. GREGORY
As pope A.D. 590-604, Gregory reformed the services of the church and arranged the music of the chants. One of the truly great popes. Died A.D. 604.

ST. HELENA (HELEN)
Mother of Constantine the Great and legendary discoverer of the true cross of Christ at Jerusalem. She built the Church of the Nativity at Bethlehem, the oldest Christian church in the world. Died A.D. 328.

ST. HILDA
Of royal blood, Hilda took the habit of a nun. Because of her piety and holy life she was soon appointed abbess. Her influence was a factor in securing unity in the English church. Died A.D. 680.

ST. HILARY OF POITIERS
Hilary was a student of rhetoric and philosophy and early became a convert to Christianity. He devoted his tongue and pen to fighting the Arian heresy and suffered banishment for his zeal. Died A.D. 368.

ST. IGNATIUS
Ignatius was bishop of Antioch in Syria. When asked by the emperor for a sacrifice to heathen gods, Ignatius refused. He was condemned and thrown to the wild beasts. Martyred A.D. 107.

ST. JOHN THE BAPTIST
HE BAPTIZED OUR LORD
"The man sent from God," the voice crying in the wilderness: "Prepare ye the way of the Lord," of whom Christ said, "Among those that are born of women there is not a greater prophet." First century.

ST. JOSEPH
Joseph was the husband of Mary, the mother of Jesus. All that is known of Joseph is found in the first two chapters of Matthew and Luke. In Matthew he is described as "a just man." First century.

ST. KATHERINE OF SIENNA (CATHERINE)
From a child, Katherine was very religious, living at home in extreme self-mortification, spending much time in prayer and meditation. Later she felt called to leave home and devoted herself to the care of the sick and other good works. Died A.D. 1380.

ST. LOUIS
King of France, a brave warrior, very considerate to his people, especially the poor. In private life, more austere and prayerful than many religious people. Leader of two crusades. Died A.D. 1270.

ST. LYDIA
A seller of purple dyes. Lydia was converted through the preaching of Paul and was baptized with her whole household. She was the first recorded Christian convert in Europe (Acts 16:14). First century.

ST. MARTHA
Martha was the hostess of our Lord in her home in Bethany. Little is known of her beyond the accounts in the Gospels. She is the patroness of housewives and cooks. First century.

ST. MARTIN
One day St. Martin saw a shivering beggar and shared his own cloak with the stranger. Later he entered the church and while bishop of Tours he converted his whole area to Christianity. Died A.D. 401.

ST. MARY
About fifth Marys are mentioned in the Book of Saints. The mother of Jesus is, of course, the outstanding character among them.

ST. MARY MAGDALEN
This Mary was the sinning and repentant woman forgiven through the love of Jesus. Appropriately, she is the patroness of pentitent women. Died A.D. 68.

ST. MARY OF CLEOPHAS
The mother of the apostle, James the Less. She was one of the three Marys who stood at the foot of the cross on Calvary. First century.

ST. MARY OF BETHANY
The sister of Martha and Lazarus, who won commendation from Jesus because of her eagerness to sit at his feet and learn of him. First century.

ST. MICHAEL
One of the archangels. St. Michael is regarded traditionally as guardian of the church and its members against the evil one. It is he who is supposed to weigh the souls of men at the Last Day.

ST. MONICA
A Christian woman, married to a pagan whom she labored to convert, together with her eldest son, St. Augustine, who became the bishop of Hippo. Died A.D. 387.

ST. NATHANIEL
Nathaniel is the name used for Bartholomew in the Fourth Gospel. He was the one whom Philip brought to Jesus and whose open-mindedness qualified him to receive additional revelations about his resurrected Lord. First century.

ST. NICHOLAS
Bishop of Myra. Tradition says that St. Nicholas went secretly to the house of a destitute nobleman three nights in succession and threw a purse of gold in the window. Patron saint of children. Died about A.D. 326.

ST. OLAF
The son of the king of Norway. As a youth he lived a wild life. Accepted baptism and as a king summoned missionaries from England to Christianize his country. Died A.D. 1030.

ST. PATRICK
A captive British boy in Ireland, Patrick escaped and was educated in continental monasteries. Later he returned to Ireland preaching and teaching the gospel and building churches. Patron saint of Ireland. Died about A.D. 465.

ST. RAPHAEL
The archangel who is the guardian angel of all humanity. He is called the "Healer of God" and is identified with the angel at the Pool of Bethesda.

ST. SIMEON
As a boy Simeon joined the community of St. John Stylites. For sixty-nine years he lived on the top of pillars within the monastery, in the exercise of religious contemplation. Died about A.D. 597.

ST. STEPHEN
The deacon and first Christian martyr, called by Luke "a man full of faith and of the Holy Ghost." Stoned to death in the first century.

ST. SYLVANUS
One of seven brothers who were persecuted as Christians under Marcus Aurelius. While his mother, St. Felicitas stood by exhorting him to remain faithful to Christ, he was cast from a cliff. Martyred second century.

ST. THADDAEUS
Also called Jude or Judas (not Iscariot). Thought by some to be the brother of James the Less and the author of the epistle bearing his name. First century.

ST. TIMOTHY
Companion of Paul on his missionary journeys, and referred to by Paul as "the beloved son in faith." Reputedly beaten and stoned to death for denouncing the worship of Diana. First century.

ST. TITUS
A convert of St. Paul, and mentioned in the Pauline Epistles as his brother and co-partner in his labors. Reputedly the first bishop of Crete. First century.

ST. VALENTINE

A priest who was active in assisting the martyrs in time of persecution. He was famous for the love and charity which he manifested. Martyred A.D. 269.

ST. VINCENT

At the age of twenty, Vincent was already an ordained deacon. With an unswerving Christian faith he underwent horrible tortures under Diocletian. Martyred A.D. 304.

ST. WENCESLAS

Duke of Bohemia. A Christian, he took over the reins of government at the time of a pagan reaction. He was murdered by his pagan brother. Patron saint of the Czechs. Martyred about A.D. 938.

ST. WILFRID (WILFRED)

A devoted bishop who traveled widely on missionary labors, establishing, building, and strengthening churches throughout England. Died A.D. 709.

ALL SAINTS

A rayed hand of God signifying divine care over the souls of the righteous.

DENOMINATIONAL SYMBOLS

DISCIPLES OF CHRIST

The red chalice bearing the "X"-shaped cross of St. Andrew was developed in 1969. The chalice symbolizes the centrality of the Lord's Supper as well as the cup of Christian self-giving for the world.

The St. Andrew's cross focuses attention on the Scotch Presbyterian roots of the church.

The red color of the chalice signifies vitality, spirit, and sacrifice.

EPISCOPAL CHURCH

The Episcopal Church shield shows a red cross on a white field. In the upper left corner are nine white crosses on light blue. The nine crosses recall the nine original dioceses represented at the First General Convention of 1789.

LUTHERAN CHURCH

The Luther emblem consists of a black cross on a red heart against the petals of a rose. It symbolizes the truth that even under a cross the heart of a Christian abides on roses.

PRESBYTERIAN CHURCH, USA

The seal of the Presbyterian Church (USA) incorporates the basic symbols of the cross, Scripture, the dove, and flames. The cross is dominant, chosen because it is the universal symbol of the Christian church. The book motif above it represents the emphasis on Scripture in the Reformed tradition. The dove affirms the role of the Spirit; the flames represent both revelation and beginning of the church at Pentecost. Beneath the image of the book, the suggestion of a pulpit is seen, highlighting the role of preaching in Presbyterian worship.

UNITED CHURCH OF CHRIST

The emblem of the United Church of Christ is based on the Christian symbol known as the Cross of Victory or the Cross Triumphant. It signifies the kingship of the risen Christ over all the world. The orb, representing the world, is divided into three parts to signify Jesus' command to "be my witnesses in Jerusalem and in all Judea and Samaria and to the end of the earth."

THE UNITED METHODIST CHURCH

The cross and flame insignia relates The United Methodist Church to God by way of the second and third persons of the Trinity: God the son—the cross; and, God the Holy Spirit—the flame. The flame also suggests the tongues of fire at Pentecost. The duality of the flame represents the merger in 1968 of The Methodist Church and the Evangelical United Brethren Church.

DENOMINATIONAL SYMBOLS

SOUTHERN BAPTIST CONVENTION
The emblem of the Southern Baptist Convention combines three elements that are rich with meaning for all Christians. The cross, the world, and the open Bible symbolize much of the work of the Southern Baptist Convention. No official interpretation is given as the symbols are meant to speak for themselves out of Christian tradition.

WORLD COUNCIL OF CHURCHES
A ship with its mast in the form of a cross is surrounded by the Greek letters: OIKOUMENE. The ship represents the members of the council engaged in a common and dangerous voyage. The Greek word means the universality of the church and its worldwide mission.

LITURGICAL COLORS

Colors are often used symbolically in the life of the church. Liturgical colors and the times at which they are used are the result of traditions and popular usage. The earliest definite knowledge of the use of specific color in the service of the church is Clement of Alexandria's recommendation of white as suitable to all Christians. The Canons of Hippolytus assign white to the clergy as becoming their office. During the Middle Ages, symbolism and meaning of various colors developed, but there was no standard use or meaning. Each cathedral developed its own use of colors.

Today, liturgical colors are usually used according to the following general scheme:

White (and also **gold**) symbolize purity or joy. Used during the Christmas and Easter seasons and on high days during the Seasons After Epiphany and Pentecost.

Purple symbolizes either penitence or royalty. Used during Advent and Lent.

Red, as a symbol of the Holy Spirit, is used on the Day of Pentecost and at other times during the year when the Holy Spirit is emphasized.

As a symbol of the blood of Christ, deep red may be used during Holy Week, beginning with Passion/Palm Sunday, and also on days when martyrs are being commemorated. Deep red is appropriate for Good Friday.

Red is suitable for evangelistic services, ordinations, consecrations, anniversaries, and homecomings; also, for civil observances such as Thanksgiving.

Green symbolizes growth. Used in the Seasons After Epiphany and After Pentecost except when other colors, white or red, are required for special days.

THE CHRISTIAN YEAR

The Sundays and special days during the Christian Year recognize and symbolize different times in the life of Christ and in the life of the church.

Advent—Four Sundays before Christmas, December 25, are designated as Sundays of Advent. This is a period of expectant preparation for the coming of Christ. **Color: Purple**

Christmas Season—The period from sunset December 24 through January 6 (Epiphany). This is a time of hope and expectancy as Christ's birth and manifestation are celebrated. **Color: White.**

Season After Epiphany—The period from January 7 through the day before Ash Wednesday, the beginning of Lent, is a time of remembrance of the visit of the Wise Men and the revelation of Christ to the world. Sundays during this period are designated as Sundays After Epiphany. **Colors: White** for Epiphany, First Sunday After Epiphany (Baptism of the Lord), Last Sunday After Epiphany (Transfiguration); **Green** for other Sundays After Epiphany.

Lent—The Season of Lent begins six Sundays before Easter, designated as Sundays of Lent, of which the sixth is Passion/Palm Sunday. Lent begins on Ash Wednesday, which comes forty days before Easter, not counting Sundays. Lent is the period of penitence and preparation for the death and resurrection of Christ. **Colors: Purple** for Ash Wednesday, the Sundays of Lent, and Holy Thursday. For Good Friday either **no color** or **deep red.**

Easter Season—The crowning season of the Christian Year begins sunset Easter Eve and extends through the Day of Pentecost, which is fifty days after Easter. Pentecost commemorates the gift of the Holy Spirit and the beginning of the Christian church. The sixth Sunday after Easter is Ascension Sunday. Easter is a time of joy in the risen Christ. **Color: White** for Easter; **red** for the Day of Pentecost.

Season After Pentecost—Trinity Sunday begins the Season After Pentecost, which continues through the day before Advent. The Sundays in this season are designated as Sundays After Pentecost. The Last Sunday After Pentecost is also called Christ the King. **Colors: White** for Trinity Sunday and the Last Sunday After Pentecost (Christ the King) **green** for the other Sundays after Pentecost.